THE SOUL'S

BOOK OF

ANSWERS®

THE SOUL'S

BOOK OF

ANSWERS®

CAROL BOLT

STEWART, TABORI & CHANG

Published in 2003 by
Stewart, Tabori & Chang
A company of La Martinière Groupe
115 West 18th Street New York, NY 10011

Export sales to all countries except
Canada, France, and French-speaking Switzerland:
Thames & Hudson, Ltd.
181A High Holborn London WC1V 7QX

Canadian Distribuition:
Canadian Manda Group
One Atlantic Avenue, Suite 105 Toronto,
Ontario M6K 3 E7 Canada

Library of Congress
Cataloging-in-Publication Data on file
ISBN: 1-58479-301-5

Cover and book design by Nina Barnett
Printed in Singapore
10 9 8 7 6 5 4 3 2 1
First printing

This book is meant to be used as an oracular tool, not as a substitute for membership in a faith community nor as a study of any religious doctrine. Neither is it intended to represent a scholarly effort in any of the included theologies. The publisher and the author of this book take neither credit nor responsibility for anything *The Soul's Book of Answers* may seem to advise, nor for any of the results of that advice.

The following abbreviations refer to different editions of the Bible:
NIV: New International Verson
ASV: American Standard Version
RSV: Revised Standard Version
NLT: New Living Translation
KJV: King James Version
NAB: New American Bible
NKJV: New King James Version
JPS: Jewish Publication Society

HOW TO USE
THE SOUL'S BOOK OF ANSWERS®

+ Hold this book closed, and for a few seconds
  concentrate or speak your question aloud.
  Questions should be open-ended, e.g.,"How
  should I face this situation?" or, "What do
  I need to do about . . . ?"

+ At the same time, riffle the pages from back
  to front with your thumb. When you feel
  the time is right, stop and open the book
  to the page where your thumb came to rest:
  There is your answer.

+ Repeat the process for as many
  questions as you have.

Nagarjuna ➤

Although [you] may attain
the possession of wealth,
remain bowed like ripe rice.

Mahatma Gandhi ➤

[An] honest disagreement [can be]
a good sign of progress.

Paul Gauguin ➤

Shut [your] eyes in order to see.

Watch what emanates from
your lips.

He who seeks good finds goodwill, but evil comes to him who searches for it.

Baltasar Gracian ➤

To play with cards exposed is neither useful, nor in good taste. Do not disclose your inner self to everyone.

Dhammapada, Canto VIII ➤

To overcome one's self is indeed
better than to conquer others.

Lao Tzu ➤

[Your] ability to accomplish the great comes from not playing the role of the great. Therefore [you are] able to accomplish the great.

Benjamin Rowe ➤

Step back and observe the energies
in larger groups . . . form appears
[in] sensible order.

African proverb (Western Kenya) ➤

Only make a bridge where there is water.

John 8:32 (ASV)

Know the truth, and the truth
shall make you free.

In those who always honor and respect [others], four conditions will increase: longevity, beauty, happiness, and strength.

I John 3:18 (NIV)   ➤

Do not love with words or tongue
but with actions and in truth.

Sogyal Rinpoche ➤

It's all right.
Don't get too excited.
In the end, it's neither
good nor bad.

Ecclesiastes 9:10 (RSV) ➤

Whatever your hand finds to do,
do it with all your might.

May there be good intentions
in the mind, so that you may
perform noble deeds.

Keep on asking and you will be given what you ask for. Keep on looking and you will find. Keep on knocking and the door will be opened.

God has given each of us the
ability to do certain things well.
Do [them] gladly.

The Tenth Guru Gobind Singh ➤

Consider the time and
the moment.

Ye should be steadfast and immovable.

Be free from all dualities and from all anxieties for gain and safety, and be established in the self.

Srila Govinda Maharaj ➤

The certainty that nothing can happen to us that does not in our innermost being belong to us, is the foundation of fearlessness.

Matthew 7:1-2 (NIV)   ➤

Do not judge, or you too will be judged. With the measure you use, it will be measured to you.

Ezra 10:4 (JPS) ➤

Arise, for the matter belongeth unto thee; be of good courage and do it.

. . . the wise [one] relinquishes the smaller pleasure in view of the greater one.

Matthew 7:13 (NIV) ➤

Enter through the narrow gate.

Hildegard of Bingen ➤

Look all around. Wherever you see dirt, wash it away and make green whatever is dry.

Nagarjuna ➤

Although you know the difference between good and bad deeds, you should carry out your work after consultation.

Proverbs 15:15 (KJV) ➤

He that is of a merry heart hath a
continual feast.

Elijah de Vidas ➤

Rise up and hasten to prepare
provisions for [t]his journey.

Jeremy Taylor ➤

Do not be overly concerned to change [others'] opinion[s].

Nelson Mandela ➤

None of us, acting alone, can achieve success.

All actions are judged by the
motives prompting them.

The Gnostic Gospels ➤

If one has knowledge, he receives what is his own, and draws it to himself.

Hildegard of Bingen ➤

Take care to carry your burden and collect every good work in the purse of your heart.

Work without attachment, then
[you will] attain the Supreme.

St. John of the Cross ➤

To come to the knowledge of all,
desire the knowledge of nothing.
To come to the knowledge you
have not, you must go by a way in
which you know not.

Chinese proverb ➤

Deal with the faults of others as gently as with your own.

Sogyal Rinpoche ➤

Let your heart go out in spontaneous and immeasurable compassion.

Baltasar Gracian ➤

Do not enter where too much is
anticipated.

Charles Dubois ➤

Be ready at any moment to sacrifice what you are for what you could become.

Know your chief asset, your great talent, cultivate it and help along the others.

Nagarjuna ➤

The invisible [will] appear before
you and again become invisible.

John 16:33 (RSV) ➤

Be of good cheer.

Chief Seattle (Duwamish) ➤

Whatever [you] do to the web
of life, [you] do to [yourself];
all things are bound together,
all things connect.

Renounce the craving for the past, renounce the craving for the future, renounce the craving for what is between, and cross to the opposite shore.

Isna-la-wica (Teton Sioux) ➤

In any great undertaking, it is not enough for [you] to depend simply upon [your]self.

Baltasar Gracian ➤

Do not exert more energy than a business warrants.

Sogyal Rinpoche ➤

You can do nothing to inspire [another] if you do not inspire yourself first.

The Unconditioned is the seed,
the Conditioned is the flower
and the fruit. Knowledge is the
branch and the Name is the root.
Look and see where the root is;
happiness shall be yours when you
come to the root . . . [it] will lead
you to the branch, the leaf, the
flower and the fruit.

Let not kindness and truth forsake thee, bind them about thy neck, write them upon the tablet of thy heart.

'Abdu'l-Baha' ➤

Endure every difficulty and
hardship with a dilated heart,
attracted spirit, and eloquent
tongue, in rememberance of
the Merciful.

Proverbs 25:9 (JPS)   ➤

Debate thy cause with thy neighbor but reveal not the secret of another.

Alan Ashley-Pitt ➤

[One] who follows the crowd will usually go no farther than the crowd. [One who] walks alone is likely to find himself in places no one has ever been before.

Ecclesiastes 5:1 (JPS) ➤

Be not rash with thy mouth.

If you can dare to be foolish,
soon the world starts revealing
its mysteries.

Confucius ➤

Hear and [you] forget. See and [you] remember. Do and [you] understand.

The Tenth Guru Gobind Singh ➤

Let self-control be [your] furnace, and patience [your] goldsmith. Let understanding be [your] anvil, and spiritual wisdom [your] tools.

Watch ye, through this your truthfulness, there in the place of spacious view.

African proverb (Ambede) ➤

If the needle doesn't pass, the thread doesn't follow.

Bhagwan Shree Rajneesh ➤

Fall back to the heart.

Hyemeyohsts Storm ➤

[You] must find [y]our Gifts among
the great Gifts.

With a tranquil heart, take aim.

Rebbe Nachman of Breslov ➤

Make every effort to increase your longing for God.

Jeremy Taylor ➤

Look with great forgiveness upon
the weaknesses of others.

The Upanishads, Brihadaranyaka ➤

As a great fish swims along the two banks of a river, in the same way, [allow your] Spirit to move along [these] two dwellings: this waking world and the land of sleep and dreams.

Yiddish proverb ➤

A wise [soul] hears one word and understands two.

Rebbe Nachman of Breslov ➤

[Y]ou are a miniature world. [Your] essence contains the world and everything in it.

What has been [your] past, that will be [your] future.

Martin Buber ➤

[Be] truly joyful, like [one] whose
house has burned down, [yet] feels
his need deep in his soul and
begins to build anew.

As cold waters to a faint soul, so is good news from a far country.

Associate with a wise friend, who detects and censures [your] faults and who points out virtues as a guide tells of buried treasures.

Sing with gladness and keep your seat unmoved within your heart.

Mold [your]self into what [you] admonish others to be.

The Supreme Spirit teaches you to be still even in the midst of all your activities.

When you speak, speak the truth; perform what you promise; discharge your trust; be chaste in thoughts and actions.

Dhammapada, Canto XXII ➤

If anything ought be done, perform
that deed with all [your] might.

Albert Einstein ▶

The most beautiful thing [you] can experience is the mysterious.

Empty [your] boat . . .
when emptied it will go lightly.

Lao Tzu ➤

[Your] deeds can be presented to others as gifts.

Bernadette Roberts ➤

Fix [y]our uninterrupted gaze on the unknown.

Bhagavad-Gita ➤

See inaction in action, and action in action. [You are] in the transcendental position, although engaged in all sorts of activities.

African proverb (Plaatje) ➤

However long the night, the dawn will break.

Plunge into the waters of goodness and learn to swim. With grace as its shore for bathing [goodness is] clear and undefiled, it soothes all who immerse themselves.

Everywhere, truly, those of integrity stand apart . . . the good don't chatter in hopes of favor or gains. When touched now by pleasure, now pain, the wise give no sign of high or low.

The Egyptian Book of the Dead ➤

Permit thou not to be judged according to the mouths of the multitude.

Nagarjuna ➤

Although you may only succeed partially, even without succeeding you are to be admired.

Nagarjuna ➤

Keep your resolves to yourself as secret, like the body which lies [hid] in the mud. If it were not that the sprout attracts attention, who would find the lotus root?

Eleanor Roosevelt ➤

You must do the thing you think
you cannot do.

The Tenth Guru Gobind Singh ➤

Prepare the ground, and then plant
the Seed of [your] True Nature.

Ralph Waldo Emerson ➤

For everything you have missed
you have gained something else.

The Wiccan Rede ➤

. . . live and let live, fairly take and fairly give.

The Buddha ➤

[Your] actions are [your] only true belongings.

Stay where you are, and all things
shall come to you in time.

Thich Nhat Hanh ➤

It is not a matter of faith; it is a matter of practice.

Gendun Rinpoche ➤

[There is] nothing to do, nothing to force, nothing to want, and everything happens by itself.

Many things which cannot be
overcome when they are together,
yield themselves when taken little
by little.

Sogyal Rinpoche ➤

You must constantly nourish
openness, breadth of vision,
willingness, enthusiasm, and
reverence; that will change the
whole atmosphere of your mind.

African proverb (Western Kenya) ➤

A broken plate cannot be rejoined.

Thich Nhat Hanh ➤

Sometimes your joy is the source
of your smile, but sometimes
your smile can be the source
of your joy.

Lift up your head and be comforted.

Thich Nhat Hanh ➤

[A] well is within [you]. If [you] dig deeply in the present moment, the water will spring forth.

His Holiness the Dalai Lama ➤

[You] have to make the effort. Contribute to others, rather than convert others. The future is in [y]our hands.

The Buddha ►

After observation and analysis, when you find that anything agrees with reason, and is conducive to the good and benefit of one and all, then accept it and live up to it.

Zen Master Dogen

See the virtues but not the
shortcomings of others.

Martin Luther King, Jr. ➤

The ultimate measure is not where [you] stand in moments of comfort, but where you stand at times of challenge and controversy.

Mother Teresa ➤

Have courage for whatever comes.

Zen Master Dogen ➤

This dewlike life [will] fade away; avoid involvement in superfluous things.

The Wiccan Rede ➤

What ye send forth comes back to thee, so ever mind the law of three. Blessed be.

All is prepared for your delight.
Live as long as life may last.

Zen Master Dogen ➤

Valuable advice often offends
one's ears.

Ramakrishna ➤

Forget all the worldly knowledge
that thou hast acquired and
become as a child . . . then will
thou get the divine wisdom.

Ralph Waldo Emerson ➤

In skating over thin ice, our safety
is in our speed.

Let your light shine before [all],
that they may see your good works
and glorify your [Creator].

Ralph Waldo Emerson ➤

Do not go where the path may lead, go instead where there is no path and leave a trail.

Peace Pilgrim (Mildred Lisette Norman) ➤

Rejoice at small gains; [don't] be impatient, as impatience hampers growth.

Lester Levenson ➤

The only limitations [you] have are the ones that [you] accept.

Lao-tzu ▶

Manifest plainness and embrace
the genuine; lessen self-interest
and make few your desires.

Serbian proverb ▶

Be humble, for you are made of earth. Be noble, for you are made of stars.

Don't speak unless you can improve upon the silence.

Bhagavad-Gita ➤

[Be] satisfied with gain which comes of its own accord, [be] steady in both success and failure.

Proverbs 27:19 (NIV) ➤

As water reflects on a face, so
[your] heart reflects [you].

The Universal form can show you
whatever you now desire to see
and whatever you may want to
see in the future. Everything—
moving and nonmoving—is
here completely, in one place.

It is better to engage in [your] own occupation, even though [you] may perform it imperfectly, than to accept another's occupation and perform it perfectly.

The Upanishads, Yajurveda ➤

Look upon all with a friendly eye.

African proverb (Sukuma) ➤

The wind does not break a tree
that bends.

Bahujan ➤

Let [your] actions be in the interest of many and result in the happiness of many.

Hebrews 11:1 (NIV) ➤

[Your] faith is in being sure of what [you] hope for and certain of what [you] do not see.

Paramahansa Yogananda

Outward longings [will] drive
[you] from the Eden within;
they offer false pleasures that
only impersonate the soul's
happiness. The lost paradise
is quickly regained through
divine meditation.

Whatever means [you] know for
calming [your] own life, that [you]
should [practice].

Your original wonder must be recaptured; just like a childlike sense of wonder, where nothing is known and everything becomes a mystery.

Baltasar Gracian ➤

Live with those from whom you can learn.

Chinese proverb ➤

If you want to know your past,
look into your present conditions.
If you want to know your future,
look into your present actions.

Do nothing out of selfish ambition or vain conceit, but in humility consider others better than yourselves. Look not only to your own interests but also to the interests of others.

Chinese proverb ➤

The [one] who removes a mountain begins by carrying away small stones.

You [are] encircled by the embraces of the divine mysteries.

Chinese proverb ➤

Keep a green bough in [your]
heart, the singing bird will come.

Lin Yutang ➤

Spend a perfectly useless afternoon
in a perfectly useless manner; [now]
you have learned how to live.

Chinese proverb ➤

That the birds of worry and care fly
above your head, this you cannot
change; but that they build nests
in your hair, this you can prevent.

If you can't go over,
you must go under.

The Egyptian Book of the Dead ➤

[Let] thy heart reneweth its youth.

Hildegard of Bingen ➤

Be steady and you will never fail.

Chinese proverb ➤

A flower in the heart blossoms
on the surface.

Jeremy Taylor ➤

Focus on the strengths of those around [you].

Yamamoto Tsunetomo ➤

With an intense, fresh, and under-
laying spirit, make [a decision]
within the space of seven breaths.

Native American Prayer ➤

Give thanks for unknown blessings
already on their way.

African proverb (Ethiopia) ➤

Do not vacillate or you will be left in between doing something, having something, and being nothing.

Japanese proverb ➤

The reverse side also has
a reverse side.

Fall out of thinking.

Do not forget to entertain strangers. For some who have done this have entertained angels without realizing it.

If you insist on too much clarity
you will lose contact with what is
real and alive.

'Abdu'l Baha'i ➤

[Experiences] do not come to
us by chance, they are sent to us
by Divine Mercy for our own
perfecting.

Lao Tzu ➤

A journey of a thousand miles
must begin with a single step.

Nagarjuna ➤

Learn to distinguish what
should be done and what not;
the clever [soul] will always select
his opportunity.

The Gnostic Gospels ➤

Seek and inquire about the ways
you should go, since there is
nothing else as good as this.

Know well the differences between work in devotion and work for fruitful results.

Be strong and put on the
armor of light.

Lao Tzu ➤

[Your] suppleness, softness, weakness, and delicateness occupy the superior position.

African proverb (Ashanti) ➤

By coming and going the bird
weaves its nest.

Lao Tzu ➤

Take actions but do not possess them; accomplish [your] tasks but do not dwell on them.

Winter, summer, happiness,
and pain; giving, appearing,
disappearing; nonpermanent,
all of them; just try to tolerate.

To come to be what you are not,
you must go by a way in which
you are not.

Heed correction, [and you will]
gain understanding.

African proverb (Zulu) ➤

Every stream has its source.

In everything, do to others what
you would have them do to you.

Meister Eckhart ➤

Treat all things as if they were loaned to you; whether body or soul, sense or strength, external goods or honor, house or hall. . . everything.

Lao Tzu ➤

Let nature take its course. By letting each thing act in accordance with its own nature, everything that needs to be done gets done.

Lao Tzu ➤

The secret waits for eyes
unclouded by longing.

Proverbs 31:8-9 (NIV) ➤

Speak up for those who cannot speak for themselves. Speak up and judge fairly; defend the rights of [others].

Lay aside caution, it cannot help
thee against destiny; to worry with
precaution is toil and moil; go,
trust in Providence, trust is the
better part.

African proverb (Bateke) ➤

The river [will] swell with the
contribution of small streams.

Giving thanks for blessings
increases blessings.

John 15:12 (NAB) ➤

Love each other as [your creator
has] loved you.

Hidden things are manifested
by their opposites.

Riches are not from an abundance of worldly goods, but from a contented mind.

A cheerful heart is good medicine.

Sayings of the Prophet Mohammad ▶

Whoever hath been given
gentleness, hath been given a
good portion in this world and
the next.

It is worse to be busy about the trivial than to do nothing.

Learn to know thyself.
He who knoweth his own
self knoweth God.

Hakim Abu' L-Majd Majdud Sana'i of Ghazna ➤

Wait for what [your] soul shall
see in sleep.

Franz Kafka ➤

Remain sitting at your table and listen...simply wait, be quiet, still, and solitary. The world will freely offer itself to you to be unmasked, it has no choice, it will roll in at your feet.

John 14:27 (NAB) ➤

Do not let your heart be troubled,
and do not be afraid.

Zuni–Native American Prayer ▶

Follow toward whom [y]our thoughts bend, with [y]our thoughts following them, this [you] shall always live.

Be strong and enter into your own body; for there your foothold is firm. Put all imaginations away, and stand fast in that which you are.

The Gnostic Gospels ➤

The place which you can reach,
stand there.

Hyemeyohsts Storm ➤

It is a flower that can be opened in many way . . . Unfold the petals of [your] stories one by one and [you] will see a great deal.

The Gnostic Gospels ➤

Recognize what is before your eyes, and what is hidden will be revealed to you.

Zuni–Native American Prayer ➤

Make your road come forth,
Make your road come hither,
Think; "Let it be here."

With the load of desires which you hold on your head, how can you be light? . . . Keep within you: truth, detachment, and love.

Proverbs 25:28 (JPS) ➤

Like a city broken down and without a wall, so [are you] whose spirit is without restraint.

You may never find the forest if you ignore the tree.

Hebrews 13:5 (NAB) ➤

Be content with such things
as ye have.

Rumi ➤

This being human is a guest house. Every morning is a new arrival. Be grateful for whoever comes, because each has been sent as a guide from beyond.

Meister Eckhart ➤

Do exactly what you would do if
you felt most secure.

By the constant fall of waterdrops, a pitcher is filled; likewise the wise person, accumulating merit little by little, becomes full of merit.

Rumi ▶

[You have] come into the world for a particular task, and that is [your] purpose.

Hyemeyohsts Storm ➤

The answer to conflict is the Give-Away. Whenever one gives from his heart, he also receives.

Navajo Rain Dance Ceremony ▶

As [you] walk, the universe is walking with [you].

[Be] like the moon: stainless, pure, serene, and unruffled.

It is more blessed to give
than to receive.

Philippians 4:8 (NKJV) ➤

Whatever things are true, whatever things are noble, whatever things are just, whatever things are pure, whatever things are lovely, whatever things are of good report, if there is any virtue and if there is anything praiseworthy—meditate on these things.

Cherokee proverb ➤

Don't let yesterday use up too much of today.

St. John of the Cross ▶

To come to the pleasure you have
not, you must go by a way in
which you enjoy not.

Baltasar Gracian ➤

Mark your words; there is always time to add a word, but none in which to take one back.

Chief Luther Standing Bear (Oglala Sioux) ➤

Never rail at the storms, the furious winds, the biting frosts and snows . . . Bright days and dark days are both expressions of the great mystery.

Cheng-Tao Ke ➤

When you seek to know it, you cannot see it. When you are silent, it speaks.

Meher Baba ➤

Don't worry, be happy.

Zen Master Dogen ➤

Focus your mind on one thing,
absorb the old examples, study
the actions of [the] Masters—
penetrate deeply into a single form
of practice.

Matthew 6:34 (NIV) ➤

Do not worry about tomorrow, for
tomorrow will worry about itself.

The Poetic Edda ➤

Enjoy the good you are given.

The Egyptian Book of the Dead ➤

[If] thy heart is fixed,
thy legs are set firm.

A tree is recognized by its fruit.

Pema Chodron ▶

It's not an accident; whatever comes into [your] space is there to teach you.

The Wiccan Rede ➤

Soft of eye and light of touch,
speak ye little and listen much.

Lao Tzu ➤

If you know when to stop, you'll suffer no harm. And in this way you can last a very long time.

The Gnostic Gospels ➤

Bring in your guide and your teacher.

Pema Chodron ➤

Develop [y]our curiosity, not caring whether the object of [y]our inquisitiveness is bitter or sweet.

Pema Chodron ➤

[The] wisdom that exists,
exists in what you already have.

The Tenth Guru Gobind Singh ➤

Nothing else can be done.

Lao Tzu ➤

Be square but don't cut; be sharp
but don't stab; be straightforward
but not unrestrained; be bright but
don't dazzle.

African proverb (Ethiopia) ➤

[Do not wait] to think of water
when the well is empty.

The Egyptian Book of the Dead ▶

Sendeth [your] heart to rule
[your] body.

Freely ye have received, freely give.

Ecclesiastes 9:7 (JPS) ➤

Go thy way, eat thy bread with
joy and drink thy wine with a
merry heart, for God hath already
accepted thy works.

Let your speech be always with grace, seasoned with salt.

African Folktale ➤

Thou must grow out, that thou mayest become like that which thou hast been.

The Wiccan Rede ➤

When ye have and hold a need,
hearken not to others' greed.

PEI Bonewits ➤

Strive to make [y]our life consistent with [y]our proclaimed beliefs.

Yiddish proverb ➤

Light is not recognized except
through darkness.

There is nothing covered that shall not be revealed; neither hid, that shall not be known.

Benjamin Rowe ➤

[Your] acts are in accord with the will of [your] creator.

Swami Chinmayananda ➤

The highest form of grace
is silence.

The Tenth Guru Gobind Singh ➤

Burn emotional attachment,
and grind it into ink. Transform
your intelligence into the purest
of paper. Make love to your
pen, and let consciousness be
the scribe.

Lao Tzu ➤

Maintain tranquility in the center.
[Even though] things come forth in
great numbers, each one returns to
its root.

Nagarjuna ➤

For the temporary but supreme gift
of words any price should be paid.

Mosiah 3:19 (Book of Mormon) ➤

Becometh as a child, submissive, meek, humble, patient, full of love.

Proverbs 3:13-14 (JPS) ➤

Happy is the man that findeth
wisdom and the man that obtaineth
understanding. For it is better than
silver, and the gain thereof than
fine gold.

African proverb (Yoruba) ➤

One who does not understand
the yellow palm bird [will] say it
is noisy.

Dr. Martin Luther King, Jr. ➤

What are you doing for others?

Proverbs 4:23 (NIV) ➤

Above all, guard your heart, for it is the wellspring of life.

Sogyal Rinpoche ➤

Throw a pebble into a pond. It sends a shiver across the surface of the water. Ripples merge into one another and create new ones. Everything is inextricably interrelated.

Proverbs 11:24-25 (NIV) ➤

One man gives freely, yet gains
even more; he who refreshes others
will himself be refreshed.

Marie Curie ➤

[You] are gifted for something
and that thing, at whatever cost,
must be attained.

Japanese proverb ➤

Fall seven times, stand up eight.

African proverb (Kenya) ➤

Put out a fire while it is still small.

Harriet Beecher Stowe ➤

Never give up, for that is just the place and time that the tide will turn.

The Wisdom of Rastafari ▶

[Don't] place [your] own
short-range ambitions ahead of
[your] long-range interests.

Mahatma Gandhi ➤

A "no" uttered from the deepest conviction is better than a "yes" merely uttered to please.

Lucretius ➤

Constant dripping hollows out
a stone.

Richard Bach ➤

Step toward expressing [y]our real nature. Everything that limits [you], put aside.

You can know [your] life through synthesis, not through analysis.

Albert Einstein ➤

Imagination is more important
than knowledge.

Marcel Proust ➤

[Your] real voyage of discovery consists not in seeking new land-scapes, but in having new eyes.

You must make the effort. The Buddha can only point the way.

Aryeh Kaplan ➤

It is not good for [you] to be alone.

Marcus Aurelius ➤

Such as are your habitual thoughts, such also will be the character of your mind; for the soul is dyed by the thoughts.

Herman Hesse ➤

Everything becomes a little different as soon as it is spoken out loud.

Unknown ➤

Go beyond logic—the world
functions in divine order.

Hyemeyohsts Storm ➤

It is through seeking that
[you] will grow.

Grandma Moses ➤

Life is what [you] make it.
Always has been, always will be.

Albert Einstein ➤

Out of clutter, find simplicity;
from discord, find harmony;
in the middle of difficulty lies
opportunity.

Theodore Roosevelt ➤

Do what you can with what you have, where you are.

Benjamin Disraeli ➤

The greatest good you can do
for another is not just to share
your riches, but to reveal to him
his own.

Mahatma Gandhi ➤

Satisfaction lies in the effort,
not in the attainment. Full effort
is full victory.

Ambrose Redmoon ➤

Courage is not the absence of fear, but rather the judgment that something else is more important than fear.

The Gnostic Gospels ➤

Bring forth what is within you,
what you bring forth will save you.

Romans 12:12 (NIV) ➤

Be joyful in hope, patient in affliction, faithful in prayer.

Choose your project carefully
and achieve it worthily.

Ovid

Let your hook be always cast;
in the pond when you least expect
it, there will be fish.

St. John of the Cross ➤

To arrive at being all, desire to
be nothing.

Franklin Delanor Roosevelt ▶

The only thing we have to fear
is fear itself.

Lao Tzu ➤

If you store much away, you are bound to lose a great deal.

African proverb (Nigeria) ➤

Sweet and sour walk hand in hand.

The Tenth Guru Gobind Singh ➤

Whatever is to be done,
the Lord is doing.

Henry Ward Beecher ➤

Hold yourself responsible for a higher standard than anyone else expects of you.

Peter McWilliams

Be willing to be uncomfortable. Be comfortable being uncomfortable. It may get tough, but it's a small price to pay.

The Buddha ▶

[Your] thought manifests as [your] word; [your] word manifests as [your] deed; [your] deed develops into habit; and habit hardens into character. So watch [your] thought and its ways with care, and let it spring from love born out of concern for all beings.

The Tenth Guru Gobind Singh ➤

Get rid of your skepticism.

Theodore Roosevelt ➤

The worst thing you can do
is nothing.

Love [all others], do good to
them and lend to them without
expecting to get anything back.
Be merciful, just as your [Creator]
is merciful.

Carl Jung ➤

Everything that irritates [you]
about others can lead [you] to
an understanding of [yourself].

Wounds from a friend can be trusted, but an enemy multiplies kisses.

Never consider yourself the cause
of the results of your activities, and
never be attached to not doing
your duty.

Proverbs 14:23 (KJV) ➤

In all labor there is profit.

Acknowledgments

This book is dedicated with much love and respect to my father and mother, Robert and Doris Bolt. They taught me, early in my soul-searching, that the world is filled with many voices and beliefs and that there is something to be valued in each one of them if only you take the time to listen respectfully. Thank you for giving me ears through which I continue to learn how to truly listen.

I gratefully acknowledge and am humbled by the wisdom of the authors of the works referenced herein, and am grateful to the Creator.

To my agents, Victoria Sanders and Chandler Crawford: I deeply appreciate your ongoing efforts and support.

To my editor, Anne Kostick; the book's designers, Nina Barnett and Galen Smith; production director, Kim Tyner; publicist, Caroline Enright; and publisher, Leslie Stoker. Thank you for the opportunity to make this book and to work with you in making it really special.

Several people directly contributed to the collection of the material that became this book. Many thanks to: Kris Caldwell, Aileen Gagney, Barbara Sewell, Lou Cabeen, David Philips, Sandra Everlasting Jones, Taen Scherer, Mondi Mallory, Jaq Chartier, Dave Caserio, all my friends at the Seattle Public Library, and the myriad of inquisitive souls and publishers of sacred texts on the World Wide Web.

Author's Note

My goal in *The Soul's Book of Answers* was to include as wide a range of traditions as possible. Some religious texts are not written in a voice that was appropriate to this context; others may not have been included simply because there was not enough time to find them.

Spiritual traditions included in this book

African traditional
Baha'i
Buddhism
Christianity
Confucianism
Egyptian Spiritual Tradition
Enochian Magickal Tradition
Hinduism
Islam
Jainism
Judaism
Mormonism
Native American spiritual traditions
Odinism
Rastafarianism
Sikhism
Sufism
Tantra
Taoism
Universal Wisdom
Wicca Rede
Zoroastrianism

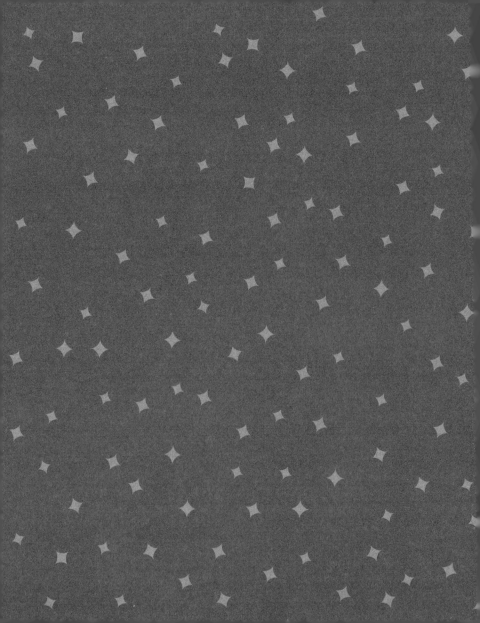